Practical Wisdom for Nurturing Body, Mind, Heart, and Soul

Vicki L. Dobbs

You First

All rights reserved. No part of this publication may be reproduced, distributed, or transmitted in any form or by any means, including photocopying, recording, or other electronic or mechanical methods, without the prior written permission of the copyright holder, except in the case of brief quotations embodied in critical reviews and certain other noncommercial uses permitted by copyright law.

Copyright © 2021, Vicki L. Dobbs, Wisdom Evolution
Clovis, California
www.vickidobbs.com

ISBN: 978-1-7373404-2-3

Cover by Thesbian (99Designs)
Proofread by Theresa Scandale
Formatted by Shanda Trofe

Limits of Liability and Disclaimer of Warranty

The author/publisher shall not be liable for your misuse of this material. This book is strictly for informational and educational purposes.

The purpose of this book is to educate and entertain. It is distributed with the understanding that the author/publishers are not engaged in the dispensation of legal, medical, psychological or any other professional advice. The content of each entry is an expression and opinion of its author and does not necessarily reflect the beliefs, practices or viewpoints of the publisher, its parent company or its affiliates. The publisher's choice to include any material within is not intended to express or imply any warranties or guarantees of any kind. The author/publishers do not guarantee that anyone following these techniques, suggestions, tips, ideas, or strategies will be successful. The author/publisher shall have neither liability nor responsibility to anyone with respect to any loss or damage caused, or alleged to be caused, directly or indirectly by the information contained in this book.

Dedication

I dedicate this book to you, the Reader,

and all the crazy busy folks out there

who just need a reminder to breathe.

Contents

Foreword vii

Introduction ix

Chapter One: Sucked into Their Drama; Setting Yourself Aside . 11

    Stone Creek Gathering 11

    Truth in the Retelling 21

    Food for Thought: Speak Your Truth! 21

Chapter Two: Start Dancing 31

    Nurture Your Body 31

    Dance, My Friends! 36

    Food for Thought: Know What Is Important to You! 36

Chapter Three: Empowering Your Stories 47

    We All Began with a Story 47

    Nurture Your Mind 47

    Food for Thought: Have Courage! 50

Chapter Four: Start Singing 61

    Nurture Your Heart 62

    Dream For You 62

    Food for Thought: Dream Big! 64

Chapter Five: The Sweetness in Silence 75

    Nurture Your Soul 75

    Food for Thought: Pay Attention to the Heart That Speaks through Longing! 78

Epilogue: Nurture Yourself Intentionally 87
Acknowledgments 95
Testimonials 97
About the Author 99
Get Your Free Gift! 101

Foreword

You First is a tiny treasure trove of stories and steps to set sacred boundaries that nourish your heart and soul. Vicki has taken years of personal wisdom and consolidated her learnings and gifts into a healing guide for spiritual seekers, artists, and creators.

In reading this little book, you will journey around a sacred wheel of self-discovery as you reconnect to the ancient traditions of singing, dancing, communing in silence, and telling your stories.

As the best-selling author of the Warrior Goddess Training series and the Warrior Heart Practice, I recognize in Vicki's words, the same energy of balance; balancing the "doing and being" parts of ourselves. I can feel into her heart and recognize how she has moved through the four chambers of feeling (singing), of intent (dancing) of truth (silence) and of story (telling yours).

You First introduces you to another way to connect with your own authenticity and nurture the truth of your own sacred being.

~ **HeatherAsh Amara** - **Warrior Goddess Mama**, author of *Warrior Goddess Training, Warrior Goddess Wisdom, The Seven Secrets to Healthy and Happy Relationships* with don Miguel Ruiz Jr. and *The Warrior Heart Practice*

Introduction

*I*f you've gotten lost in a life of doing for everybody and everything else except for yourself, here are some helpful hints and daily insights designed to show you simple ways to nurture yourself, intentionally caring for your body, mind, heart, and soul.

You have a right to be happy. In *You First*, I share my own experiences through story and offer you simple practices for taking care of you while you are taking care of all your responsibilities.

This book came about after I found myself metaphorically buried in the pile of broken plates that had fallen from the sticks I held up, trying to keep them all spinning in my world. I picked myself up, swept up the mess, and got back in the game, intentionally devising a plan to take care of me first.

After reading this book, you will be empowered to put YOU FIRST, inspired to take care of yourself, know that when life gets out of balance, when all those spinning plates begin to wobble and fall, you will have practical, real-life exercises to bring you back to you. If you don't take care of yourself, you can't take care of anyone or anything else in your life indefinitely. Let's put YOU FIRST and use the included journaling pages to document your journey as you step into living an intentional life, one where you matter. You have a right to be happy.

Note:

There are little "snacks" offered as Food for Thought at the end of each chapter. They are to inspire you to think for yourself, to ponder the story, and to consider the questions posed.

Journal your answers on the following pages and contemplate what each morsel of that "Food for Thought" might be feeding you. Write your days, write your dreams, write away what no longer serves you, write a new story that empowers your journey, draw your heartsong, doodle creatively, paint your secret pleasure or scribble incoherent poetry.

Use the "extra" pages to play, dream, draw, doodle, let go, release, reimagine, and be grateful. Remember the "F" words in your life – Faith, Family, Fun, Fitness, Finances and Friends and journal them into your journey.

If you find yourself set aside, come back to you by filling these pages with your desires, your joy, your pain and your pleasure, what made you feel good and what sucked, be grateful and feel good.

Blessed be another day!

Chapter One
Sucked into Their Drama; Setting Yourself Aside

*E*ver find yourself at a place where you have planned something just for you, to invest in yourself, only to have your time turn south as you get sucked into someone else's drama?

This is a story written nearly twenty years ago after I attended an event at a rustic desert retreat. I wrote it to remind myself that it is OK to put me first, to say no when a yes doesn't serve my best interest, and that it is OK to say yes when it is said with joy and grace, not frustration and doubt. I have changed my name and the names of my friends and even the time, historically, of my experience, to create a "story" to share the lesson I learned and continue to learn on this earth walk.

Stone Creek Gathering

"Let's go, let's go!" she shouted as she bounded around the corner of the tent. Elaina had been napping after lunch, under a huge sycamore tree down by Chilkoot Creek. She wasn't a stone's throw from her campsite, but she hadn't been paying attention and now it was nearly time for the first meeting at this annual Stone Creek Gathering. Running back to her tent, Elaina found her friend Marni wasn't ready either; she was moving about aimlessly, acting like she was gathering her things for the afternoon meeting. Elaina and her best friend Genise started off without her.

"Oh wait!" Marni yelled, "I'll just be another minute."

Frustrated but feeling like it was important to be together, Elaina and Genise waited while Marni finished getting ready. They made their way to the central meeting grounds and quietly took their places in the back of the room filled with women waiting, singing, and drumming in anticipation of their teacher's arrival.

Winded from the last-minute rush, Elaina found it hard to quiet down and concentrate. Several deep breaths later, she vowed softly not to let herself be distracted like that in the days ahead. This was the annual meeting of her people. They came every year to listen and learn, to journey for their own personal insight and spiritual messages, and to meet themselves in a higher place in the process.

The girls—Elaina, Genise, and Marni—had met at this event the year before. They had run into each other searching for a place to set up camp and decided it would be easier to camp together in one large tent rather than separately in small ones by themselves. They all lived in the western part of the country, one by the ocean in the north, one in the desert to the south, and the third in a valley centrally located between the other two. They shared the love of this gathering and the things they learned here and had made plans to camp together again this year.

The first meeting ended as evening came, and dinnertime was fast approaching.

Everyone would gather around a central fire area to share a

buffet style meal. The three girls made the hike back to their campsite to get ready for dinner. They changed clothes, washed up, and gathered the food they had brought to share. Elaina had been wearing sandals with her denim skirt and more than once had stubbed her bare toe on a rock along their path. "We should change quickly and get back," Elaina said, trying to motivate the other two to get a move on. Putting on her soft leather boots, she reminded Marni and Genise, "You know how fast the food goes. If we are late, we will just have leftovers to pick through for dinner."

Marni was busy redoing her flaming red hair and Genise was packing food.

"We have plenty," Marni scoffed back as she went to change her skirt. She loved "being seen" and wore bright colors made into flowing skirts that bounced around her when she danced about the campus. Genise and Elaina both dressed in simple fashions, although Genise always wore beautiful jewelry—big silver earrings, and a necklace that usually matched her clothes.

"I'm ready," Genise called out as she carried the bundle of food out to Elaina's wagon.

It was a hike from the girl's campsite back and forth to the meeting areas. Elaina had brought her wagon this year, remembering how long it took to cross the huge span of the campgrounds last year. She asked her friends if they would like a ride, and of course their voices echoed a unanimous yes in the evening quiet.

The girls worked together to hitch the wagon to Elaina's little pony, Jilly, and they headed off to dinner, laughing as they bounced over rocks scattered over their path.

Someone's dog bounded up and jumped into the wagon with the girls and out again, as it saw a rabbit across the field and took chase. Giggling together, Elaina asked Jilly to hurry it up a bit as she gently slapped the reins across Jillie's fanny in encouragement.

So many people had gathered this year. There must have been 150, maybe 200 men and women, all milling around the evening fires, visiting and nibbling, enjoying this first meal they were all sharing together.

Elaina left her friends and walked over to a group of girls she hadn't seen since last year. They laughed and talked while they ate, catching up on the past year before going on to the night meeting.

When the late gathering was over, Elaina looked around for her two friends, Marni and Genise, not seeing them anywhere. She hadn't seen them since dinner when Elaina left with her other friends. She got in her cart and drove her little black pony slowly back to the eating area, hoping to find them. No one had seen Marni or Genise since supper. Elaina headed back to their tent at the campgrounds down by the creek.

Shortly after she had settled in for the night, the other two girls showed up, tired and upset with her for not waiting to give them a ride back. Elaina explained that she did wait and that she had looked for them. She told them that she even went back to the eating area and couldn't find them. The three agreed they would meet at the big eucalyptus tree on the far side of the eating area after meals. It was along the path to their gathering spot, and they could go together from there to the meetings.

Elaina grumbled quietly under her covers, *"I'm not waiting. If they don't show up on time, I'm just going to get myself to the gatherings alone."* The voice in her head was telling her differently, telling her she would give in and wait anyway, knowing she wouldn't want to disappoint anyone even if it made her late.

She sighed and drifted off into an unsettled, restless sleep. Now Elaina was tied down to being a shuttle service for her friends. When would she have the time to explore, to visit her other friends, to sit in silence in this wonderful place, on this sacred land at Stone Creek? Her sleep was restless that night, fitful and filled with unremembered dreams that teased her throughout the night.

The next morning the three girls were up with the sun and took a quick dip in Chilkoot Creek. It was a little quieter stream of water that branched off the river known as Stone Creek. The waters of Chilkoot formed a natural pond just below an 8-foot waterfall spilling over giant boulders and piles of rocks. It was the perfect place to bathe or swim or just be in the water.

Elaina recharged herself in the pool. Water always brought her back to a sense of balance, a place of remembering herself with the water's unconditional support. This morning she needed it; she was tired from her lack of sound sleep, and there would be so much to do today. She allowed herself a few extra minutes to float and release her tension to the water, relaxing into that floaty place from which she could just drift away and be in that moment.

Back at their campsite, the three of them loaded the wagon, hitched up Jilly, and headed off to breakfast. Elaina and Genise took their packs and all they would need for the first meeting that morning and for lunch as well. Marni hurried out of the tent at the last minute and joined them as their wagon began to roll down the dirt road to breakfast. Marni was winded and agitated again as Elaina and Genise had not waited for her.

They tried to explain that they were not going to wait anymore, that if Marni wanted to ride to the eating fires or even to the meeting flats, she would have to be ready when the rest were, or she would have to walk on her own.

Elaina hated confrontation and the ride to breakfast was one wrapped in uncomfortable silence. She left Jilly tethered to the eucalyptus tree near where they all ate and wandered off by herself, carrying her pack in readiness for the morning gathering. She wanted to get there early and find a good place to sit where she could see and hear her teacher. Today she promised she would take whatever time she needed for herself to relax and to get the most out of this year's gathering.

The day went well. Elaina had done what she wanted, when and where she wanted, without giving up any more time worrying about her companions. Sunset was approaching. Back at their campsite, Elaina hadn't seen Genise or Marni all day. She decided to get her pony and ride to a hilltop to watch the sun set. She could feel the need to sit alone in silence and voice her gratitude for the day's lessons. Elaina unhitched Jilly and just as she was riding away from the evening fire, she heard someone yelling her name. She turned and it was Marni running after her.

"Where are you going?" she inquired. "Can I come along?"

Reluctant but unable to say no, Elaina waited while Marni caught up and climbed up behind her on Jilly. Arguing with herself under her breath, Elaina grumbled, *"Why can't I just say no? I hate it when people look disappointed or upset with*

1 | SUCKED INTO THEIR DRAMA; SETTING YOURSELF ASIDE

me. Then I feel bad, get upset with myself, and my insides churn all around the 'yes,' making it so uncomfortable for me, but I say yes anyway."

When they arrived at the top of the hill, Marni jumped down and began gathering stones and setting up a sacred circle, calling in the directions and waiting for Elaina to join her. Elaina brought her drum and a small flute, respectfully entering the circle Marni had created. She sat down in the center, faced the setting sun, closed her eyes, and began to play, letting her mind drift with the notes her flute sang. Marni interrupted and asked her to drum while she danced the sun down, singing her own song, the words unknown to Elaina.

With a deep sigh and a knot twisting in her belly, Elaina put down her flute, picked up her drum, and began to rhythmically tap out a cadence for Marni to dance to. Even Elaina's drum was not happy and voiced her discomfort with a tight, twanging, tinny sound. All Elaina could think about was why she had said yes to Marni's request to come along in the first place.

The evening didn't turn out to be anything at all like she had imagined. As the sun set in the west, silhouetting the trees and the cactus across the dusty desert hills, Elaina vowed to herself that she would learn how to say no without guilt. She had overheard a couple of new girls talking at their last meeting. "Why can't people just make up their minds and say yes or no?" one of them had asked. "I watched the craziest thing at dinner. There was this group that kept pushing one of the girls to do something she didn't want to do. You could tell how uncomfortable she was. She kept trying to say no but the others weren't hearing her. They just pushed back saying to her, 'It'll be OK,' or 'Just this time,' and things like that."

"Too many people won't take no for an answer without causing a big scene," the other girl answered. "And if you don't stand up for yourself, you'll get walked all over."

"Such a perfect message for me to overhear tonight," Elaina thought to herself. *"I'm going to practice boldly standing up for myself, stating my own wants and needs firmly, and I will hold tighter to my own personal boundaries. No more giving in to the constant barrage of requests and demands from others,"* she swore to herself.

It would take a lot of practice to change this habit of setting herself aside with a yes, when, for her, the no would be better. *"She would learn to put herself first"*, she thought to herself.

The last day of the gathering arrived. Elaina and Genise had agreed the previous night to get up before dawn and walk out into the desert to watch the sun rise. Marni heard them stirring and sat up asking, once again, if she could come along. Elaina let out a sigh and a weak "fine," but Genise firmly answered, "If you can be ready to go right away! We are leaving in a few minutes and we are not going to miss the rising sun on our last morning here."

Elaina and Genise finished packing their backpacks and were heading for the tent flap when Marni exclaimed, "Wait, wait, I am coming!"

Genise shouted back that they were not waiting, and, taking Elaina by the arm, she pulled her out of the tent. Elaina was consumed with guilt almost immediately and questioned her friend about them not waiting just a bit longer for Marni.

"Do you want to see the sunrise?" Genise asked. Elaina nodded her head yes. "Then we must go!" It was that simple.

"We have given in to her being late all week, and I am not going to do it anymore. If you want to give up the sunrise to wait for her, go ahead. I'm not. I am leaving." With those words, Genise flipped the tent's flap down and stomped off.

Elaina thought for about a half a second, and then, quietly thanking Genise for showing her what taking control of her own time looked like, the two of them set off across the desert in the bluish gray dawning of this last morning that they would have together for another year.

They found a rocky hill just made for climbing and picked their way to the top in time to see the sky change from gray-blue purple and pink to firelight orange, then fade into the soft blue sky of dawn. The shadows of the rocks below them began to stretch out as they crawled across the sandy ground with the rising sun. The desert took on a pastel blanket of pink and peachy colors that quickly turned to golden shades of amber then yellow as the sun climbed over the hills into the eastern sky. What a magnificent play of colors and shadow dancing that, if Elaina had waited just that minute more for Marni, she would have missed.

Elaina and Genise placed sticks on the top of the hill that they had decorated with pieces of ribbon and woven with blades of grass collected around the campsite. With Genise singing softly in the background, Elaina spoke aloud, "I vow to take back the power to control my time. I have given it away to all the people in my life. No more! I accept responsibility for my own actions, for those yes decisions when I wanted to say no, and I realize that in waiting on others to share my experiences, I am diminishing my own." She let out a long sigh, knowing this was a big step in her life, one she thought was worth taking.

YOU FIRST

The rising sun cast a shadow westward from the prayer sticks they had just planted. Elaina felt a death deep within her, the passing of this need she had lived with for so long, this need to please others and make sure they were happy for her to enjoy, or perhaps validate, her own experiences. She envisioned that lengthening shadow carrying away her need for other people's happiness to be her burden. Without thinking, she pulled the bone-handled knife from its sheath on her belt and made a slashing movement through the shadow of her prayer stick even as it began to shrink with the rising sun.

Elaina looked over at Marni standing quietly in the morning light, a smile spreading across her face. "Way to go, my friend!"

That morning in the newness of the rising sun, Elaina had found within herself a place of welcoming awareness that she was all she needed. That within her was all she had been, was now, and would ever be.

Turning to her friend Genise, Elaina placed her hand over her heart and then waved it palm up and outward toward her friend, Genise signaling her heartfelt gratitude for mirroring to Elaina the strength she had within her own self.

Facing the now risen sun, Elaina bowed in thanks, then straightened and raised her arms to face the morning sky in gratitude for the beauty of this unfolding day and the two friends who had been her greatest teachers at this year's gathering.

Elaina and Genise made their way back to the final meeting of this year, to the last time with their teacher and to all the farewells they would share with their family of friends that gathered here each year. Elaina was taking home a newly remembered piece of herself she had long ago given away. She had gifted herself permission to say no and to allow herself to be first before the wants and needs of others.

The year to come would be a new experience Elaina would face with herself, by herself, and for herself. She picked up a small, pinkish-red-colored stone lying beside the wheel of her cart as she moved around to hitch Jilly for the drive home. Putting it in her pocket, she thought she would place it on her altar, remembering each time she saw it the beautiful sunrise that had gifted her such a powerful message, and her dear friends who had helped her remember it was OK to say no.

Truth in the Retelling

The story of Elaina and her experience at the Stone Creek Gathering is the truth of one of my own challenges. I realize in retelling it here that in those times of saying yes when I want to say no, when the shadow dwellers push forth all their negativity, they are telling me that it is time to get out of that situation, to stop doing for others, and to take time to do what I want and need to do for me.

Food for Thought: Speak Your Truth!

Make a conscious effort to connect to your truest desires, your own inner voice and spirituality without fear of judgment from yourself or anyone else. Freedom comes to you when you stand in your own authenticity. When I was asked to support a venture a friend was starting, I wanted to say yes, but my whole body was telling me no. My heart was racing, my stomach was alive with butterflies, and my head pounded like I was inside a drum someone else was playing. I was filled with the desire to do something for and with her, but my heart and common sense were telling me that it was not right for me. I took a deep breath and gently said no without a long-winded explanation that would have had me circling back to the possibility of saying yes.

It takes courage to say no. It often takes more strength to say no than it does to say yes. It is OK to say no. Use your yeses, intentionally.

1 | SUCKED INTO THEIR DRAMA; SETTING YOURSELF ASIDE

The first step towards meaningful change is awareness... Who controls your Yeses?

YOU FIRST

Today joy found me in the golden glow of the *morning* light...

1 | SUCKED INTO THEIR DRAMA; SETTING YOURSELF ASIDE

Where did you dance today?

YOU FIRST

My heart found joy in the darndest place…

1 | SUCKED INTO THEIR DRAMA; SETTING YOURSELF ASIDE

I stood up for me today when…

YOU FIRST

Today, I am *Grateful* for...

1 | SUCKED INTO THEIR DRAMA; SETTING YOURSELF ASIDE

Doodle away! It's OK to play… *and have* FUN!

Chapter Two
Start Dancing

*I*n these so-often trying times of change, of transformation and new beginnings, it is more important than ever to pay attention to your body, to your physical presence, in each day.

Are you aware of how you interact with your world throughout the day, even each moment of each day? Most people aren't. Are you making conscious decisions, or are you moving through your days like the proverbial hamster running on its wheel, just getting from one thing to another in hopes of getting everything done? That's how I was—shuttling kids from one activity to another, self-employed Realtor, volunteering, taking care of family and animals. How many plates are you currently spinning in your physical world? Like in my case, there may be too many to keep them all in the air.

I'm here to help.

Let me tell you another story.

Nurture Your Body

"When is enough, enough?" I asked myself. I was pregnant and my doctor had just made a joke to my girlfriend Susan and I. We were both pregnant and going to the same doctor, so we scheduled our appointments together.

"Two pounds a month, girls," he laughed, then seriously continued, "Not two pounds a week."

Pregnancy was my first experience with excessive weight gain. I loved being pregnant and so did my body. I had no morning sickness, no discomfort to speak of, but I did balloon up. At that time, ultrasounds weren't routinely done, and the doctor thought part of the weight was that I was having a big baby. I don't think that accounted for much of the sixty piled on pounds.

I didn't eat consciously. I ate like I always had, when I wanted to and what I wanted to eat. In the three years since college graduation, I had been more sedentary, less active. I had a desk job for a couple of years, cookies in the drawer, soda on the desk. I was building my own business doing custom leatherwork, again, at a desk-like workbench.

After the baby came, nursing was easy, and I loved it. I don't think I ever put Ryan to bed awake. I spent hours with him, blessed to be able to stay home and work rather than leave him with a sitter. I remember buying that first pair of after-baby jeans and how shocked I was when I realized that the waist measurement exceeded the inseam length. When I got pregnant, I wore 32"/36" Wranglers, and now I was buying 38"/36".

Post-partum depression wasn't talked about much back then. I don't really remember feeling bad, just feeling empty, even lonely. Ryan didn't sleep a night through 'till he was nearly seven years old, and I was the only one getting up every night, off and on, all night long.

I joined a weight loss group about a year later, and with a little conscious effort, the weight came off, just in time for the next pregnancy.

2 | START DANCING

When you pay attention to what you eat and what you drink, and when you are drawn to food or drink, you may connect that consciousness to an event, action or even emotion that comes up during the day. Do you make choices that serve you and your truth, not ones that necessarily just make you feel good? If you choose the feel-good foods when you feel good and want something yummy to eat beyond your usual fare, it becomes a mini celebration of you each day rather than a habit you are feeding for some other reason. Think about the choices you make and when you make those choices. Whatever they are, give yourself permission to eat and drink intentionally.

I went in for a routine annual checkup not long after our daughter went off to college. Dr. Heinrichs jokingly asked if I was pregnant. "No way," was my reply, "You took care of that for me the year after Raney was born."

Gene thought that my uterus was larger than he thought it should be and sent me off for an ultrasound. Long story short here, they found an ovarian cyst the size of a grapefruit and sent me off to an OB-GYN who took one look at the reports and scheduled surgery for the following week, telling me that if that cyst ruptured, I probably would not have time to get to a hospital. He also explained that there were fibroids on the inside and outside walls of my uterus and that, given my age, the best plan of action for optimal health would be an ovarian hysterectomy. And so it was.

"I don't think I can go on like this. No, I know I can't," I explained to my OB-GYN, Dr. Smith. "I haven't slept more than a couple of hours in any stretch since the hysterectomy. I totally get why they use sleep deprivation as a form of torture. I am crying at the silliest things on TV. I can go from zero to bitch in under 10 seconds, like someone just flips a bitch switch, and I don't have any control over any of it."

His reply left me drop-jawed and silent. "Why didn't you call me? Your hormones are simply out of whack. We need to get them into balance, so we'll just adjust your estrogen prescription."

"How in the Sam Hill was I supposed to know?" I thought to myself furiously. "I've been in a tortured state for two weeks," I replied. "None of your follow-up literature or instructions mentioned any of these symptoms or that if they occurred, I should call in." This gray-haired, six-foot-two, mild mannered physician just looked at me with a quizzical, sympathetic expression while he wrote out a new prescription.

I hadn't had good or even healthy sleep patterns since my first child was born.

Maybe I never have. Given the chance, I'm a night owl. I've always stayed up late and struggled to get up. Add in a second child and my system was used to waking up every couple of hours, but I always went back to sleep. After the hysterectomy, I would be so tired, I couldn't keep my eyes open, but sleep wouldn't come. Then throw in the horrendous hot flashes and mood swings and my world was spinning me out of control. *"Why didn't I just call in?"* The thought of those words even now frustrates the bejesus out of me.

Do you have a regular sleep habit or pattern? Do you fight sleep when you go to bed or embrace slumber? Do you have a routine that puts you into sleep mode when you go to bed, or do you just end the day after you brush your teeth and jump between the covers?

2 | START DANCING

Sleep is the great restorer. It is necessary for boosting your immune system, strengthening your heart, increasing productivity, and improving memory. Getting enough sleep can help reduce stress and put you in a better mood. I know, for me, lack of sleep leaves me grumpy, irritable, and unable to connect with my day.

According to WebMD, a good night's sleep allows you to process your emotions. I think it even heals your heart. Refreshing slumber helps you hit the reset button on a bad day, improve your outlook on life, and be better prepared to meet challenges.

Begin to pay attention when you go to bed. Are you sleepy or is it just that time? Are you napping during your favorite evening TV show? What is your body telling you? Do you love an afternoon nap?

When you put your conscious effort into developing a good habit around sleep, it will be easier to fall asleep. You will sleep better when you sleep intentionally.

Take a few minutes every hour or two and pay attention to your breath. My watch alerts me to breathe and gives me the choice to take a few moments and do just that. Inhale deeply, hold it for a moment, and slowly exhale, even if it is just once in that moment. Wherever you are, you can spend a few minutes doing some sort of intentional breathing exercise if you choose to.

I like to do this one in the car; the red light is my beacon, my reminder to breathe. Additionally, it keeps me from getting impatient, slows me down, and I know this to be true; it makes me a better, more consciously aware driver. Watching TV is another great opportunity to center yourself with your breath.

Try this at your desk or on an evening walk—count breaths. Inhale slowly counting one, two, three, four. Hold it one, two, three, four, and exhale slowly releasing one, two, three, four, and repeat.

Whatever works for you, do it intentionally. Breathe.

Dance, My Friends!

Movement is a crucial part of taking care of you, so dance, my friends. Move in whatever form that takes for you. Dance across the kitchen floor to the refrigerator and back to the sink. Dance down the hallway when you get up in the morning. Allow yourself opportunities to move and cherish that ability to move. Wiggle your fingers and your toes, run across the yard, or do a walkathon, plant vegetables or flowers, bench press your grandchild's tricycle or the soup cans in your pantry. Whatever way you choose to move each day, as many times a day as the thought pops into your mind. Work or play, move intentionally.

Food for Thought: Know What Is Important to You!

Identify your core values; not the inherited voices, not your monkey-mind chatter but your true values, the truth of YOU. They are the guiding principles that dictate your behavior, how you perceive right and wrong. These core values represent your highest and most deeply held beliefs, your life priorities, and are at the very core your fundamental driving force moving out in your world.

What lights you up? Are you familiar with the old saying, "If it feels good, do it"? When you are aligned with your own authentic truth, doing what you want to do and what fuels your fire, it feels good. That is your truth speaking through your body-mind, letting you know you are in alignment with the truth of you. Make your choices intentionally!

YOU FIRST

Dance (like no one is watching), dance through your day, movement is play...

2 | START DANCING

What five things did you do to move today - to intentionally *breathe* today?

"You have to eat, you have to move, you have to breathe..."
~ Susie Powder

One day at a time, one step at a time, one breath at a time, I can...

2 | START DANCING

Freedom found me with, in, on…

What *sparked* your hero's journey?

2 | START DANCING

List some of your core values...

What lights you up?

YOU FIRST

Today, I am *Grateful* for...

2 | START DANCING

Doodle your dance, doodle your breath. Doodle the day and play…

Chapter Three
Empowering Your Stories

We All Began with a Story

"Where did you come from?" a friend asked me one day.

"What do you mean?" I asked, "I came from home. Why?"

"No, not today," he replied. "Who are your people? Where do you come from?"

Jubel was Native American, and his question reminded me of my friend Isabelle's introduction of herself when she and I first met at an event in New Mexico. She told the group her name, then introduced herself with her native name, her clan, and her tribe, where she was from. Dr. Lewis Mehl-Madrona, MD, is a Native American author, speaker and professor. He tells the importance of your story and speaks to this way of introducing one's self in his audiobook, *The Spirit of Healing*.

Nurture Your Mind

Here's some of my story. I came to be, thanks to the United States Army Air Corp. My father was a staff sergeant in the supply division sent to an office to gather requisition forms. My mother was the secretary in that office.

They loved to dance, and the rest is history as they say. They married in Missouri during World War II. Daddy was from St. Joseph (home of the Pony Express), and Mom was reared in Greenfield where her grandfather was a nurseryman. Her father fought in the trenches in France in World War I.

The Army transferred my folks to California in 1946. They lived in Shell Beach for a while and then Daddy was transferred to Chandler Field in Fresno. My mom got a job as a bookkeeper. My sister was born in 1947, and in January of 1949, they bought a house. Several months later, I arrived.

I moved to Clovis in 1969 (less than 10 miles from the home I grew up in), and my parents followed from their first house, in 1991. I graduated from college and married in 1972, had two children and lived over 40 years in the same home, moving in 2019 just five more miles away from where I began. I guess you could say I've been around here my whole life.

Throughout the world, indigenous peoples have relied on the power of story to share and retain their history, the creation stories of their people, and the chronological history of their families. Storytelling is an integral part of their healing process. It is, perhaps, the defining characteristic of being human.

Our stories and the way they are told and interpreted, are how history is revealed and remembered. We inherit our parent's stories as we learn what we live growing up with them, and then we get to write our own.

My dear friend Ila shared with me one day at lunch, as I was telling yet again, the story about the trauma and family dysfunction that surrounded the loss of my son. Ila gently reminded me, "Vicki, your story doesn't have to define you. You can keep telling the same story over and over again, or you can choose to change the story."

That's the treasure I want you all to read here today. It's time for you to acknowledge that you are the artist of your life, the author of your own story, and at any given moment, *you* can change it.

Create a new one that ignites your life and stop living the one that extinguishes it. Our stories can be reshaped, reborn, and rewritten with inspiration from life, friends, teachers, books, or movies. Listen, watch, and capture that golden nugget that will change the story you are living.

Here's how to get started. Read a favorite book in your comfy chair or out on a blanket on the lawn. Find the works of writers that entertain as well as inspire and inform. Read intentionally.

Write when you can, what you can, where you can. Journal regularly or journal when the mood strikes. Scribble down sparks at Starbucks or at the doctor's office.

Talk to your phone recorder while you enjoy a glass of wine or when you retire for the evening. Write for breakfast, lunch, or dinner. Wherever you write, whatever you write, whenever you write, gift yourself your own wisdom and write your stories intentionally.

Tell your stories, the uplifting and powerful ones and the hard and hurtful ones, the ones that taught you your greatest lessons, the ones that made you who you are today. Talk to your children, their children, your friends, and even strangers.

Ask your parents and grandparents to share their stories with you. I wish my family had talked more or I had taken the time to ask more questions. I wonder now about their lives, their struggles, their triumphs, but they are gone, and they didn't talk; they didn't share their history.

Whatever brings you alive is what you should follow. Pay attention to the stories that ignite a giggle or bring a tear; they are trying to teach you something.

When we stop telling stories, our stories, we cease to inspire, inform, and entertain. When we stop telling stories, we open the door for discomfort and dis-ease. Don't stop sharing your story; someone out there needs it. It could change their life.

Speak aloud your stories and talk intentionally.

Teach what you know, what you have lived. Teach the young ones and teach the elders; it is never too late to learn. You are a unique expression of the Divine walking on this earth, at this time. Allow yourself the gift of learning that comes with teaching, and teach intentionally.

Food for Thought: Have Courage!

"Courage is the most important of the virtues because without it you can't practice any other virtue consistently." ~Maya Angelou, Black American poet, memoirist, and civil rights activist, author of *I Know Why the Caged Bird Sings*

It takes courage to voice our authentic selves, not what we think we ought to say but the truth of our souls. Have the courage to ask this question, "What lies in the bottom of my heart?"

When I put that question to myself, when I looked deep into the flame of my heart's desire, I heard that still, small voice from Spirit whisper softly, "Write, play, create, and teach intentionally."

YOU FIRST

Write your day, today or change it… just write a story, or *imagine* a play…

3 | EMPOWERING YOUR STORIES

Where do you come from?
What is your creation story?

What story will you tell someone else today, your friend, child, grandchild? *Share* you...

3 | EMPOWERING YOUR STORIES

Jump off into the realm of all possibility… start a new story today.

YOU FIRST

Who can you talk to today, ask questions, hear their story?

Write that story as if you were teaching a lesson to your child.

_____
_____
_____
_____
_____
_____
_____
_____
_____
_____
_____
_____
_____
_____
_____
_____
_____
_____
_____
_____
_____
_____
_____
_____

3 | EMPOWERING YOUR STORIES

What was your big ah-ha today?

YOU FIRST

Today, I am *Grateful* for...

3 | EMPOWERING YOUR STORIES

Draw the story or your play, let you imagination loose and have FUN today!

Chapter Four
Start Singing

Someone on the TV just said, "Stop beating yourself up and be kind to yourself." That brought my thoughts up short and pulled my attention back to me, out of the endless chatter on TV.

"I can't believe how sad I am today," I thought when I heard that. My heart felt like a lead weight in my chest at times, it was even hard to catch my breath. *"Oh crap,"* I wondered to myself. *"Am I getting this global bug that is devouring the energy of the world?"*

"Don't be silly!" I scolded myself out loud and remembered the quote taped on my computer by 13th-century Persian poet and scholar, Rumi:

"That which is false troubles the heart, but truth brings joyous tranquility."

My head was beginning to buy into all the "stuff" being spouted hourly out of the "boob tube," even though I didn't think I was paying attention. *"I'm fine,"* I reminded myself. *"Move into your heart and check out what is going on,"* that familiar voice reminded me.

Nurture Your Heart

I set my phone down, closed my eyes, and took a few deep breaths. I moved my consciousness purposefully down into my heart and listened. I looked about and could see how constricted the walls looked. I could feel the "sad" energy here, and I asked quite simply, "Why?"

"You've lost your dream," my heart answered. "You have forgotten You. That is the source of your sadness. Forget about all that is going on around you, around the country, even around the world. Come back to you; remember at the heart of you is your dream, and you must remember your dream. The sadness will leave when you replace it with the inherent joy that is carried on the wings of your dream."

It felt like my heart skipped a beat and then it was lighter. The walls softened, and, with a deep breath, I felt it expand, to begin to radiate love and joy, to fill with light. I took another deep breath and opened my eyes. Even the room seemed lighter, felt brighter. My body loosened and my shoulders dropped. "Inhale your dream and remember..." the voice trailed off. "Remember."

Dream For You

Do you have a dream? Did you know you can have a dream, that you have a right to be happy, to dream "happy" for yourself?

Set aside time to dream. I don't mean your nighttime dreaming. I mean time to DREAM, dream you, who you want to be, how you want to be, and what you want to be doing. Practice being excited. As Beth Beurkens—a life coach, spiritual

4 | START SINGING

healer, and one of my teachers—would say, "Is your heart happy?"

Try starting an "I'm Happy" journal. Make a conscious effort to take a little time every few days or even once a week and check in with you. Ask yourself this question, "Is my heart happy? If not, why?" Write it down; begin a new journey.

"You all have a story, but you are all much more than just your stories," Beth would say. "You all have history, but you are all greater than just your history. You are connected to the power of the Infinite, connected to the above and the below. There is nothing missing in you. You are one with this Universal Presence."

Sing in glorious harmony with the Universe of All That Is. Dream with it; ask it for whatever your heart desires. Decide not just what you want but how and when to ASK FOR IT! Most of us are accustomed to giving. Allow yourself to receive and dream your wildest desires into reality. Dream intentionally.

Let love in; give voice to your soul's song. Open your heart to all the wondrous love that surrounds you every day. Pay attention to the little things that make your heart flutter. Doesn't it soar just a bit when you are gifted the smile of a child in the grocery store or the wide-eyed adoration of your puppy or cat, when you hear your favorite song or see a longtime friend in town?

Put your shoulders back, drop them, and let them fall away from your ears as you expand your rib cage with a big, deep breath, and allow the space around your heart to grow.

What are you grateful for today? Each day find something that you are thankful for. Bless that gift—be it a spring flower or the winter snow. Love them equally. Try something different and embrace change as an opportunity to love something new. Pay attention to the things that bring spontaneous tears to your eyes. That is your heart loving openly. Above all else, love intentionally.

Release what is no longer healthy or serving you in a positive way. Do you recognize the voice of someone else chatting in your ear? Is there a constant dialogue going on in your head about things that should have been, could have been or would have been?

Let go of yesterday. As Beth would teach, "That was then (swipe it away), and this is now (bring it present)!" Write it away before you go to sleep if the loop is still playing through your mind. Let go of all those inherited expectations. Let them fly on the wings of a paper plane or float away in a balloon. Send them away, release them, and let them go, intentionally.

Your healing begins when you move past the ignorance you have allowed to rule your heart. Be curious and lead with your heart. You'll find your answers, your dream, when you dream with your heart, intentionally.

Food for Thought: Dream Big!

Open your life to creativity and playfulness instead of fencing yourself in with lackluster limitations. Don't let your rational mind shut down your dream before it even has a chance to soar. See it, then BELIEVE it.

I have found for myself that when I share my plan or goal with someone else, when I give them permission to hold me accountable for my dream, then I pay more attention to it myself. A great dream deserves support and encouragement. Don't be afraid to ask for it and be open to it. My friend and writing coach Dawn Montefusco would tell you, "I don't believe in a God that would give you a dream and not the means to manifest it."

Give voice to your heart's song. Sing intentionally.

Is your *heart* happy?

That which is false troubles the heart, but truth brings joyous tranquility." ~ **Rumi**

4 | START SINGING

You have a dream… Sing it aloud to the world.
List what you need to manifest it!

Today I begin to release, let go of and dissolve what stands in the way of my dream…

4 | START SINGING

Today I felt the beauty of...

YOU FIRST

I felt the *beauty* in...

4 | START SINGING

Is your heart happy today? Open your heart –

give voice to your soul's song.

YOU FIRST

Today, I am *Grateful* for...

Activity and play - doodle your day and draw the dream, write your song or just sing along.

Chapter Five
The Sweetness in Silence

Nurture Your Soul

I'm one who usually doesn't go somewhere new unless I have someone to go with. I'm also not likely to do new things without someone to do them with. Several years ago, I took myself hiking, by myself, while visiting Sedona. I flew to Phoenix, rented a car, and drove the two hours to Sedona. I found a boutique hotel, checked into a room with a fireplace and a jetted tub, and vowed I would not turn on the TV or my music for the whole weekend. I was going to test this silence thing and see if it was something I could do for more than a few minutes.

That evening I went to the store for food so I wouldn't be tempted to go out or do the fast-food thing. I found fruits and cheese, deli meats, and a sweet treat or two.

Heading to the checkout, a book caught my eye. It was called *Hike Sedona*. I hadn't planned on hiking as I was not in the greatest physical condition, but this book labeled the different hikes as easy, moderate, or tough. I figured I could do easy.

The next morning, I took off early, ahead of the pink Jeeps and the noise of excited tourists. I hiked indigenous ruins in the silence of the first light after dawn, and what magic I found in it. I heard the voice of wisdom whispering in my ear, watched the hawks circle, and heard the song of the cottonwoods harmonize with the creek. There was such peace in that silence.

The hustle and bustle of the tourist arrivals sent me to find new trails. Not only did I make easy, I conquered moderate that day as I stacked stones in the back of Boynton Canyon. I found a new me that could be alone and try new things. I found a connection to the natural world that spoke volumes as I listened and journaled its stories. I was awakened in the sweetness of silence.

One of the gifts I received in Sedona was the power of creativity. To know me is to know that I make drums and rattles, I paint, I weave baskets, I bead feathers, and I write. In silence, my creativity soars when my mind is uncontained by conventional thoughts.

When was the last time you found yourself in silence? Were you uncomfortable, looking for something to turn on or to do? Is silence scary or do you wait for those precious moments when you can embrace the sweet silence that holds quiet, ancient mysteries?

I had never spent time with myself in silence, or at least not intentional silence. There was that "be still" kind of silent time we all have in school, work, church. Being still and in the sweetness of silence are very different. It can be a profound experience, a time of sweet surrender to the magic and mystery held within.

Find a time and place where you can meet yourself in silence. Light a candle and create something that makes you smile; write, draw, paint, plaster, mold clay, sticks, or stones, Makes no difference; play. Creativity is food for the soul. Create intentionally.

5 | THE SWEETNESS IN SILENCE

The conversations I had with myself hiking turned into walking prayers with the Divine. How could one not turn to God in the majesty of these monumental creations carved out of red rock? The universal presence of the One, the Creator, God/Goddess, the Infinite by whatever name you choose, permeated every step I hiked and enveloped me with every breath I took. I heard the ancient drums sing throughout the valley.

Find the sweetness in silence. Pray daily, several times daily; let each breath be a prayer, each step be in gratitude. Prayer can be a solemn quest for assistance, or it can be expressed in gratitude. Prayers are the poetry of our souls offering our voice to God, the Divine Creator, Source of All, the One in all its names and forms. Trust in the power of your words and thoughts and pray intentionally.

Divination is you searching. Never give up on finding more, being more. Divine, discover, go in search of all that is you and all that you want to be. When you go within to divine the true source of you, that authentic piece of you that is waiting for you to claim it, live it, be it, you are searching for yourself within the unknown, the "mystery," from the seen and unseen sources, through the process of divination. Divine intentionally.

At the start of each day, set out on your hero's journey, an adventure, a treasure hunt for inspiration and clarity. Make new friends. Use any roadblocks you encounter as opportunities for learning and fight off the shadows that try to darken the day. You will return with a new perspective. You will find clarity, clear away the energy that blocks your creativity, and open your heart through the gifts you discover in the sweetness of silence.

Search out what you want to do or do for someone else, and be guided by your own revelations, motivated by your own desires, and encouraged by your own dreams. Be open to divine inspiration and listen to the silence, intentionally.

Food for Thought:

Pay Attention to the Heart That Speaks through Longing!

> *"In spite of the difficulties and frustrations of the moment, I still have a dream."*
> ~Rev. Dr. Martin Luther King Jr.,
> Minister and civil rights activist

The feeling of restlessness, that pulling, is your heart looking for its place of belonging.

Find small daily braveries, spots of time to remember that this life is holy, that you are holy. We become what we pay attention to, and the purpose of life is to live and to create, to align ourselves with God, with the Divine Great Spirit, Infinite Source, because that is what our Soul is here for.

Ask, dream, know, speak, design, welcome, go for it, learn, be courageous, and pay attention.

Take some time out of your busy-ness to have a conversation with a rock or a listen to the song of the leaves playing with the wind. Open your "ears" and listen to the whispers in the wind and babble of a brook.

Now is the time for you to TURN INWARD as much as you SEARCH OUTWARD. It is time to trust yourself, your feelings, and your dream. Trust intentionally!

5 | THE SWEETNESS IN SILENCE

Write away your day… remember each small daily bravery, remember and be *courageous*.

That was then (wipe it away)...
this is *now* (bring it present)!" ~ Beth Beurkens

5 | THE SWEETNESS IN SILENCE

What *roadblocks* did you encounter today?

YOU FIRST

Where were you challenged to keep You first?

_____
_____
_____
_____
_____
_____
_____
_____
_____
_____
_____
_____
_____
_____
_____
_____
_____
_____
_____
_____
_____
_____
_____
_____
_____
_____

Share your day, your dreams, your goals and *aspiration*...

YOU FIRST

Today, I am *Grateful* for...

5 | THE SWEETNESS IN SILENCE

Give yourself permission to doodle your day and have FUN!

Epilogue
Nurture Yourself Intentionally

With all life gives us, its ups and downs, demands, responsibilities and ever-changing landscapes, it can create a sense of dis-ease and dis-connection. If you are feeling this way, take a closer look at each of these questions posed by ancient medicine people when they were approached for assistance.

> *"When did you stop dancing? When did you stop singing? When did you stop being enchanted by stories? When did you stop finding comfort in the sweet territory of silence?*
>
> *"Where we have stopped dancing, singing, being enchanted by stories, or finding comfort in silence is where we have experienced the loss of soul.*
>
> *"Dancing, singing, storytelling, and silence are the four universal healing salves."*
>
> ~Angeles Arrien, *The Four-Fold Way: Walking the Paths of the Warrior, Healer, Teacher and Visionary*

Give yourself permission to nurture *You*,

all aspects of you.

YOU FIRST

Remember to sing...

EPILOGUE

Remember to dance...

Remember to listen for the Whispers in the Wind, to relish the sweetness in Silence...

EPILOGUE

Remember to tell your stories...

YOU FIRST

Remember you matter... that you are worthy and put YOU FIRST!

EPILOGUE

Gratitude is your Golden KEY...

I am grateful for...

_____
_____
_____
_____
_____
_____
_____
_____
_____
_____
_____
_____
_____
_____
_____
_____
_____
_____
_____
_____
_____
_____
_____
_____
_____

Acknowledgments

My basket of gratitude overflows.

I am thankful to so many for their guidance, support, and encouragement as I began this journey called writing.

I am grateful most of all, for my family, who stands back and allows me the freedom to pursue crazy ideas, lofty goals, and whimsical dreams. I couldn't do this without their love and support.

I would not be writing without the encouragement of the indomitable Kate Pistor (aka Kathryn Fleming), poet, artist extraordinaire, and friend. Go Tigers!

To my dear friend, teacher, and mentor, Lynn Andrews, thank you for the courage to step onto this Path of Heart and just go for it!

To Glenda Jacobs, whose personal journey back into herself inspires me daily.

To Dawn Montefusco, whose support and direction helped me own my voice and become a better writer.

And to HeatherAsh Amara, who walked with me to the edge of the fire and showed me "I can."

For all your encouragement, support, and energetic edits. Love you guys.

I am grateful for you all!

Testimonials

In the two plus decades I've known Vicki, she has gone from an acquaintance to a dear friend, has found herself, her voice, her writing spirit, and her creative soul. In her book, You First, Vicki introduces you to her real-world stories with practical exercises that remind you of the importance of putting you first, a lesson we should all take to heart.

~**Lynn Andrews**, New York Times and International Best Selling Author of the "Medicine Woman" Series, Founder of the Lynn Andrews Center for Sacred Arts and Training and Shaman Mystery School, The Way of the Wolf at LynnAndrews.com

I love the three words, "ancient future wisdom." We are currently reimagining life on planet eARTh together, drawing from our past and visioning into a new future that is informed by indigenous cultures and their wisdom. In "You First," Vicki Dobbs has masterfully woven together a story and a practice for each of us that can help us to thrive right now. You and I can commit afresh each day to honoring the basic principles she shares in this book to help us to rise above the heaviness and co-create a more loving and sustainable future. This is a must read!

~**Whitney Freya**, Inspired Living Expert at WhitneyFreya.com

YOU FIRST

In these pages, women of all ages will find inspiration to step into personal power, to listen to the inner voice and latch onto the courage to change.

Vicki Dobbs shares a delightful mixture of mystical storytelling and motivational coaching here that will give you the transformational jumpstart you are looking for.

A trusted guide, Vicki speaks from a deep and authentic well of love and experience.

~**Beth Beurkens, M.A**.
Shamanic Teacher, Vision Quest guide and award- winning Author of Shamans Mirror at BethBeurkens.com

About the Author

Vicki L. Dobbs is an artist, author, mentor, and coach. She is an inspirator of everyday awareness and instigator of spontaneous stories. Gratitude and grace sprinkled with humility and humor are the medicine she carries out into the world.

Vicki offers collaborative workshops and classes integrating ancient wisdom, techniques, and tools with modern modalities in an environment of experiential learning. Her teachings are the result of an evolution of wisdom that comes through her from all the sacred teachers she has been blessed to learn with on this earth walk. She follows a Path of Heart, bringing these sacred teachings to everyone everywhere who has the desire to enhance their own personal or professional spiritual journeys.

Vicki Dobbs is a teacher, writer, friend, a crafter of sacred art and tools, and a connoisseur of creativity. Join her You First Revolution at WisdomEvolution.com

Get Your *Free* Gift!

Wake up and write. Journaling YOU FIRST, first thing in the morning (or anytime you feel a need to plug in). Give yourself the gift of intentional awareness as you journal. Use this gift as a daily opportunity to connect and calendar the "F" words in your life: faith, family, fun, fitness, finances, and friends. Live an intentional life and bring yourself front and center in your day-to-day living, consciously aware of putting YOU FIRST.

This gift shows you how to:

- Come back to you each day.
- Connect to the important things in your life.
- Journal your day intentionally aware of your world, putting YOU FIRST.

To get your free pdf (printable) copy of *Journaling You First:*

Please visit www.vickidobbs.com and click on Free Gift.

BONUS GIFT: Look for my Meditation for Centering link on the thank you note.

May you always find an abundance of love, laughter, and joy in every day. Let your weeks be filled with giggles and grins, romance and friends but most of all, let your life be driven by you and for YOU FIRST!

May Spirit Bless Your Journey,

Vicki

You have a right

to be *happy!*

www.ingramcontent.com/pod-product-compliance
Lightning Source LLC
Chambersburg PA
CBHW070940080526
44589CB00013B/1583